YOUR BODY

THE ULTIMATE LETHAL WEAPON

GW01032705

YOUR BODY

BODY

THE ULTIMATE LETHAL WEAPON

KEITH D. YATES
6TH DEGREE BLACK BELT

PALADIN PRESS
BOULDER, COLORADO

Also by Keith D. Yates:

The Complete Book of Taekwon Do Forms

Warrior Secrets: A Handbook of the Martial Arts

Your Body—the Ultimate Lethal Weapon
by Keith D. Yates
Copyright © 1987 by Keith D. Yates

ISBN 0-87364-438-7
Printed in the United States of America

Published by Paladin Press, a division of
Paladin Enterprises, Inc., P.O. Box 1307,
Boulder, Colorado 80306, USA.
(303) 443-7250

Direct inquiries and/or orders to the above address.

All rights reserved. Except for use in a review, no
portion of this book may be reproduced in any form
without the express written permission of the publisher.

Neither the author nor the publisher assumes
any responsibility for the use or misuse of
information contained in this book.

Contents

About the Author

Keith D. Yates is recognized as one of the nation's leading authorities on the martial arts. He has written over twenty-five magazine articles for numerous publications, including *Sports and Fitness*, *Black Belt* magazine, *Inside Karate* and *Karate Illustrated*. He contributed the chapter on karate for Prentice Hall's sixth edition of *The Physical Education Handbook*, a widely used text in colleges and universities. His first book, *The Complete Book of Taekwon Do Forms*, is considered a classic reference text. His second book, *Warrior Secrets: A Handbook of the Martial Arts*, has been honored by becoming assigned reading in several college martial arts courses. He has also written *Just for Kicks: The Art of Fighting with Your Feet*. His fourth book, just released, is titled simply *Korean Karate* which he co-authored with a former United States Olympic coach. Mr. Yates is currently working on additional books on the subjects of self-defense, stick fighting, and one-step sparring techniques.

Starting his Tae Kwon Do (Korean karate) training in 1965 at the age of fourteen, Mr. Yates became one of the youngest black belts in the country when he earned his rank at seventeen from former world champion Allen R. Steen, "The Father of Texas Karate." After a successful tournament career (winning the state championship in 1971), he embarked on a study of other martial arts. He has trained in several styles, earning a 1st degree black belt in Japanese Ju-Jitsu and a 2nd degree belt in Okinawan Kobudo (the art of ancient oriental weapons.)

He began the first college "karate for credit" program in the Southwest in 1972 at Southern Methodist University, where he still serves as an adjunct professor. Recognized as an outstanding instructor and innovator, he is in constant demand as a seminar leader and guest teacher. He was also recently voted into the Third Edition of *Who's Who in American Martial Arts*. Mr. Yates is currently one of the highest ranking American-born masters in the art of Tae Kwon Do, holding a 6th degree black belt.

He is the founder and president of the *Southwest Tae Kwon Do Association*, an organization overseeing independent karate clubs at several YMCAs, recreation centers, and colleges. The STA teaches the "American Chung Do Kwan Style" of Korean Karate, a system founded by Mr. Yates. It is based on the traditional Korean style but with added emphasis from a number of different martial systems.

In 1986, the Texas Black Belt Commission was organized by Keith Yates. At the initial meeting, he was elected the first Chairman of the Board of Directors. This association is unique among martial arts organizations because it represents several different schools and styles. The TBBC has already gained national recognition from several major martial arts publications and is fast becoming the recognized regional accrediting organization for North Texas martial arts instructors.

Mr. Yates is currently teaching at the Richardson YMCA and at Southern Methodist University. For futher information on classes or for seminar information, please contact the *Southwest Tae Kwon Do Association* at 3402 Ridgemoor, Garland, TX 75042.

Acknowledgments

Dedicated to my students who have helped me
refine my teaching skills.

Photography by Arnold Howard, Dave Edmondson,
Bob Woerner, and Toby Threadgill

Models: Jennifer Branch, Bryan Robbins, Bruce Gay,
Bob Woerner, Keith Yates

Introduction

In the time it will take you to read this introduction, several muggings and beatings will occur and at least one rape will have taken place in the United States. Amazingly, one U.S. household in every five has been hit by crime in the last twelve months, with either property stolen or a member of the household a victim of violent assault. Contrary to what someone might say, attacks on you or your loved ones can occur anywhere and at anytime.

The incidence of crime is perhaps one reason the number of martial arts schools in this country has more than tripled in the last decade. Hundreds of thousands of men, women, young, and old are studying karate, tae kwon do, judo, and the like. These once-secret oriental disciplines are a study in personal life-saving techniques to be sure, but many students find their training to be a fun sporting activity and a healthy hobby as well. It is a mentally stimulating challenge and an effective means of physical and emotional discipline.

Most people, however, take to the mat initially out of a desire to learn how to protect themselves. The purpose of this book is to introduce you to a number of ways to defend yourself when you must do so. Of course, no written source can take the place of a reputable instructor; if you read carefully and study each technique, though, you will certainly begin to understand what you can effectively do should you find yourself in that "once in a lifetime" situation.

The techniques shown here may seem so simple that you think you can remember them without too much practice. Resist the temptation to skim over them, and spend some time becoming familiar with each. Some are so easy that you can almost master them just by simple study while others require repetitious practice over a period of several weeks so the skills will become automatic enough to be really useful if you ever need them.

This is one reason I recommend you attend actual karate or tae kwon do school. Most of us don't have the discipline to learn or practice something on our own. You don't have to sign up for a lifetime "Black Belt" course. A four- to six-month course should be enough to develop your basic habits of self-defense.

People always ask me what art to take up for self-defense purposes. Although the art itself is less important than the instructor, I'll give you a brief rundown of the differences between the various arts styles.

Basically, the arts can be divided into **grappling** and **striking** styles. Grappling arts are much like Western wrestling; throwing styles such as judo and aikido would be among the arts that fall into this category. Striking arts are more like boxing with the addition of kicks; kung fu, karate, and tae kwon do are all considered striking styles. Jujutsu falls somewhere in between these two categories, containing both throws and strikes.

So, which is better? After studying several different styles for many years, I have seen that the grappling arts generally take longer to learn than do striking styles. It just makes sense that it will take longer to learn how to throw a two-hundred-pound attacker over your shoulder than to kick him in the kneecap. For that reason, you are probably better off seeking out a karate, kung fu, or tae kwon do school first. However, I'd certainly point out that if there is a judo or aikido school in your neighborhood, you should go check it out and talk to the instructor to see if he or she will be willing to give you a brief course containing some effective self-defense techniques. In fact, no matter what style you may be interested in, be sure to check out the instructor to determine how easily you can work with him or her.

Checking out the instructor and school becomes even more important when you consider that there are no standards for martial arts schools in this country. Any green belt with three months of lessons can buy himself a black belt and put an ad in the yellow pages proclaiming himself a "master" and former world champion. The only way you can verify someone's ability is to talk to them and observe them firsthand.

But getting back to the purpose of this book, I encourage you to read and reread each chapter and try to visualize how the techniques can be applied to a number of different situations.

If you have a partner to practice with, all the better. Actually experiencing the feel of hands around your throat or having your arm twisted behind you is vital so that you won't be caught off guard should a mugger really attack you. You might even try rigging up a punching bag from an old duffel bag stuffed with old sheets or rags to actually get the "feel" of punching something with solid force.

Once you get ready to practice, it is a good idea to warm up with a few jumping jacks and toe touches. Such a warm-up can prevent muscle pulls and is good for getting you in better physical condition. After all, if you are in shape, it is easier to perform the best self-defense technique of all, running away!

You may have heard the stories about a karate expert having to warn a person three times before he can defend himself or that he has to register his hands or feet as lethal weapons. These are mere myths resulting from some overactive imaginations. You are within your rights, legally and morally, to defend yourself to the best of your ability.

A word of caution, however. Be sure you are *really* threatened. Merely having someone call you a dirty name does not give you the freedom to kick his knees or poke his eyes.

There have been cases where the victim of an attack has actually been sued because he or she injured the attacker. It is unfortunate, but you may have to prove that you were actually in danger or that at least you *believed* you (or your loved ones) were in danger and that is why you resorted to violence.

The best rule of thumb is to just walk away or try to talk your way out of an altercation. Use your common sense. After all, the other person may have a weapon in his pocket. He might have two or three friends around the corner. You don't want to fight unless you absolutely have to. Avoiding a confrontation is always a win/win situation.

I like to use this simple formula to teach my students about the importance of common sense in self-defense: **P-R-E-F.**

P is for *prevention*. This means doing things like parking under a streetlight in the shopping-mall parking lot when you know you will be returning to your car after dark. It means putting your wallet in your pocket sideways so that it is harder for a pickpocket to slide it out.

Prevention is taking some commonsense precautions to avoid any possible trouble. Don't pull out a roll of bills in a bar where you don't know anyone. Don't let a repairman in the front door without proper identification.

R is for *recognition*. Be aware as you walk down the street and you'll notice that suspicious-looking person following you. Recognize that the drunk at the bar is getting out of hand and excuse yourself before you wish you had. Recognition is being aware enough to head off potential trouble before it gets too bad.

We have all been told to drive defensively, watching out for the other guy. You should conduct yourself in the same watchful, defensive manner at all times.

E is for *escape*. This means talking your way out of a fight or running if you have to. There is no shame in running from a fight. You may have saved someone (either yourself or the other person) some serious injury (or worse) by doing so.

Cooperate with an assailant. Give him your wallet. Apologize for cutting him off on the freeway. Let him know you don't want to fight him. Remember, you want to avoid the confrontation.

F is for the actual *fight*. This part of the equation is the last resort. You only stand and fight if it is obvious he is going to beat you up, or worse.

If and when it becomes necessary to take this last step, fight as hard and as fast as you can. Have no mercy because you can be sure your attacker will have none on you. Use the most effective techniques you can, and keep hitting until you have subdued the attacker or until you can escape.

This is especially hard for women to do. They must commit themselves psychologically at that point to doing whatever is necessary to defend themselves. That may mean breaking an assailant's knee, gouging his eyes, or whatever. You must be prepared to go all the way or you will lose.

Target Areas

We're going to divide the parts of the body into thirteen target areas. The success of your techniques will depend upon striking the proper area. Not all parts of the body are vulnerable to attack, and so you must know where—as well as how—to strike. Hitting someone in the shoulder, for example, may only serve to make him more violent.

Here are the three primary target areas as taught by most self-defense instructors. These are areas which can be injured with little more than the force of a fingertip strike. A hard blow to any one of the three could be fatal, so you must be careful and use common sense if you decide to strike one of these areas.

3 Primary Targets

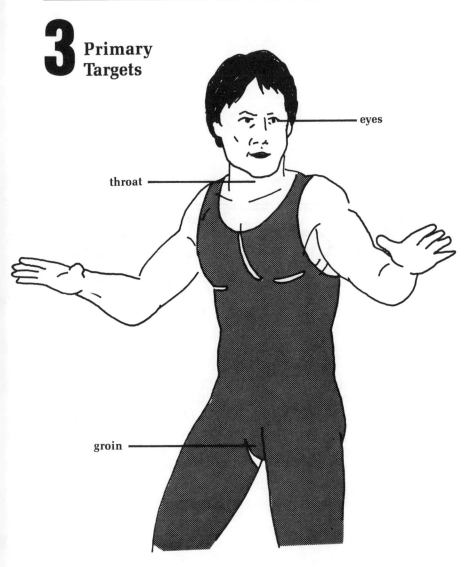

eyes

throat

groin

There are many more parts of the body that are susceptible to attack. Rather than create a long listing that you probably won't remember, I'll just point out ten of the most common and the ones easiest to get to. Let's call these the secondary target areas. Striking these targets will usually result in at least a stunning effect and, at the most moderate, serious injury.

10 Secondary Targets

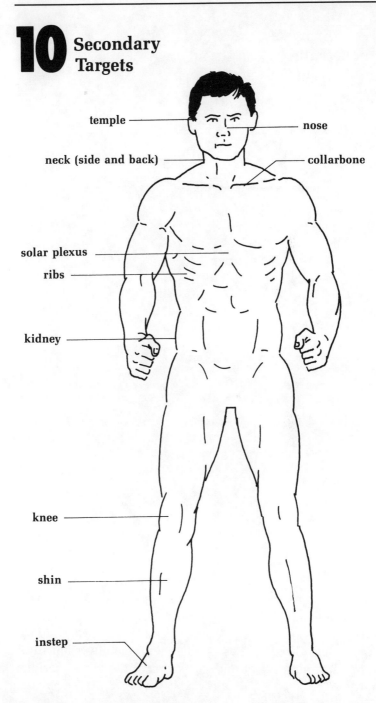

temple

nose

neck (side and back)

collarbone

solar plexus

ribs

kidney

knee

shin

instep

Basic Blocks

Any book on self-defense should cover the basic ways to block an incoming strike. After all, if your attacker hits you first and manages to knock you out, the fight is over. You need to know how to block or parry his attack. Having said that, however, blocks are actually less important in real street situations than they would be in a karate competition. Most real-life fights do not involve blocking a continuing series of blows with the hands and/or feet. A person will more often than not take a few swings at you and end up trying to grab you and throw you into a wall or over a bar. This is where you really need to know how to elbow, knee, and poke his eyes.

Being able to block well enough to stop everything an attacker might throw at you means you have spent long, long hours in practice drills. These are hours that the average person doesn't have the time or the desire to spend. So let's just cover five simple ways of blocking (and one way of standing ready). Practice them until you think you have the general concepts of movement, and don't forget to review them periodically. They may not be as important as the strikes, but remember that if he knocks you out first, you'll never have that chance to front-kick his solar plexus.

OUTSIDE BLOCK

1. This is probably the most commonly used block in a real fight. Use it to stop a swinging-type punch coming toward the side of your head.

2. The forearm does the blocking. Lift the elbow slightly so the fist cannot hook around your arm and still hit your head.

3. Note that the defender has also shifted his head to the side to further avoid the punch.

1

2

3

4

INSIDE BLOCK

4. This block is also designed to stop a swinging-type punch.

5. The opposite side of the forearm is used.

6. The same shifting of the head is employed to get further out of the way of the punch attack.

5

6

RISING BLOCK

7. This block is commonly used to stop a weapon, but it can be used against an empty hand attack as well.

8. Be sure to block the attacker's arm and not the stick or knife itself.

9. It is very important to move the head to avoid the attack especially if there is a weapon involved.

7

8   9

LOW BLOCK

10. This is used to stop either a low punch to the abdomen or a kick to the midsection.

11. Use the outer forearm to block.

12. This time, move your hips slightly to the rear to provide a safety margin as you block.

10

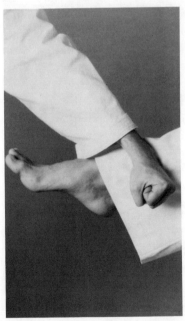

11

12

X-BLOCK

13. If a particularly large person is doing the striking, you might want to use both hands to block.

14. The same thing applies to a kick.

15. Remember: If the attacker has a weapon, you need to avoid it with your body and block as well.

13

14

15

16

DEFENSIVE POSTURE

16. If you want to maintain a defensive position without actually putting your hands up in fists (thereby signaling the aggressor that you are ready to fight), you might try this position.

17. Note how easy it is to move the hand into an outside block.

18. You can also quickly strike to the face area.

17

18

Basic Strikes

Your body is made up of a number of "weapons." A martial artist makes use of at least nine body parts (the hands, feet, elbows, knees, and head) and can turn any one of them into lethal weapons. There are a variety of ways to strike with each of these weapons. We can only cover twenty-two of them here, but if you practice enough to feel comfortable with even just a few of the ones shown in this book, you will have come a long way toward being able to defend yourself.

CLOSED HAND STRIKES (PUNCH)

How to Make a Punch

19. To make a fist, start with the fingers extended.
20. Curl them back over the palm.
21. Fold the thumb tightly over the fingers.
22. The striking surface should be the two largest knuckles.
Caution: If you hit with the little knuckles, there is a good chance you could break them.

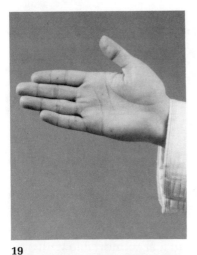

19

20

21

22

Jab

23. A straight jab is an effective technique.

24. If you don't lean into the punch, you rob yourself of power and reach.

25. By moving your hips forward, you can do much more damage. Note that the feet did not move any closer than in the previous photo; the forward thrust is done only with the hips.

23

24

25

Reverse Punch

26-27. A reverse punch is used when you need more power than a straight jab. It comes from the back side where you can use more body motion.

28. Again, you must make use of hip motion to maximize power. Shown is a weak punch that may not even reach the target.

29. Here the hips are twisted. Note that the feet did not get any closer than in the previous photo.

26

27

28

29

Inverted Punch

30. The inverted punch is used for attacking the ribs.

30

Illustration 3.   Because the fist is turned upward, the arm will bend when blocked and the fist can still reach the target area.

Backfist

31. The backfist is a powerful technique.
32. The back of the first two knuckles is used to strike.

31

32

Hammer

33. Hammer fist attacks are especially good for women and children who may not be used to striking with their knuckles.

34. The inside flat part of the hand is used to hit the desired target.

35. Close-up of the hammer fist attacks.

33

34

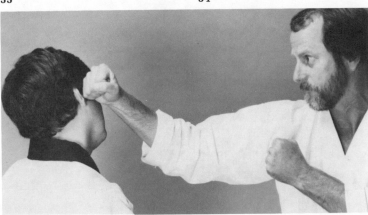

35

OPEN HAND STRIKES

Chop

36. Everyone has heard of a karate chop, more correctly called a knife-hand.

37. The striking surface is the side of the hand.

38. Note that the fingers are bent back out of the way and the thumb is tucked in.

36   37

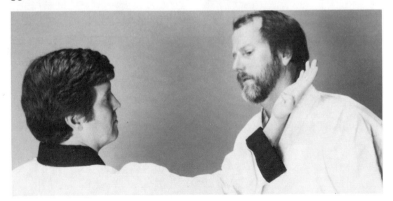

38

Ridge Hand

39-40. This is another powerful technique frequently seen in competitive karate but also useful in self-defense. The elbow should raise up as you prepare to deliver the blow to help generate maximum power in the swing.

41. The striking surface is the inside part (or thumb side) of the hand.

42. Close-up of the ridge hand.

39

40

41

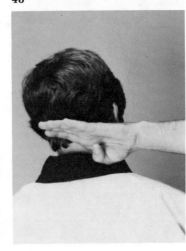

42

Palm

43. A palm heel strike is especially effective to the chin or under the nose.

Fingers

44. One or two fingers to the eyes will incapacitate an attacker.

45. If you desire to strike with all four fingers, separate them in the middle so they can straddle the bridge of the nose.

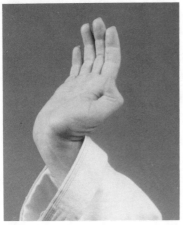

43   **44**

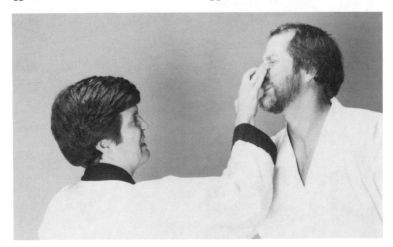

45

Tiger Mouth

46. This can be a deadly blow if done with maximum power. The windpipe could be crushed, and the person would then suffocate.

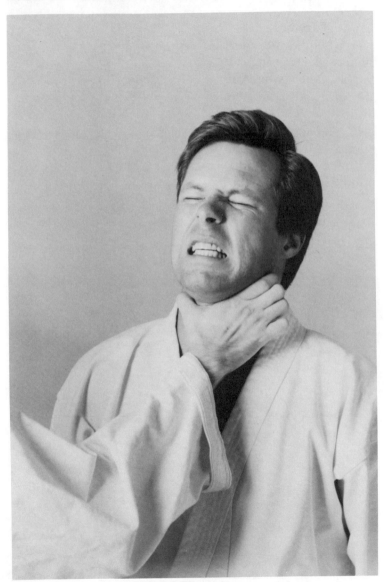

46

ELBOWS

Forward

47. This is the most often used elbow strike. It can be applied when you are grabbed from the front.

48. The actual striking surface is the flat part of the elbow and not the point or tip of the bone.

Rising

49. A rising elbow is also very effective.

47

48   **49**

50

Back

50. When someone grabs you from the rear, a back elbow is called for.

51. You can strike low with the attack...

52. ...or higher.

51

52

Down

53. A downward elbow strike is often used after a kick.

54. The kick bends the opponent over, and you can come down from above him.

55. The target areas are the back of the neck or spine.

53

54

55

FOOT TECHNIQUES

Front Snap Kick

56. Start in a normal upright position.
57. Bring the kicking foot up to the opposite knee.

56   **57**

58. The kick extends straight out to the target. Pull the toes back, and strike with the ball of the foot.

59. Snap the foot back to the original position. This is important as it increases the power of the technique and prevents someone from grabbing your foot.

60. You can also strike with the instep or with the top of the foot to the groin area.

58

59   **60**

Side Snap Kick

61. Start in a normal position.
62. Fold the kicking foot up to knee level.

61   62

63. Strike with the heel of the foot. Pull the toes back out of the way.

64. As on the front kick, retract the foot quickly in a snapping motion.

65. A kick to an attacker's knee is devastating and easy for most beginners to do.

63

64

65

Roundhouse Kick

66. Normal stance.

67. Come around with the hip and point the knee of the kicking leg toward the desired target area.

66   67

68. The kick snaps out, striking with either the ball of the foot (as in the front kick) or the instep.

69. Snap the foot back to the hip to prevent the opponent from grabbing your leg and to add to the snapping, "concussion" effect.

68   69

Stomp

70. Stance.

71. Fold the foot as in the other kicks.

72. The stomp or kick itself should travel in a downward motion toward the knee or instep of your attacker. A stomp to the top of the foot can be very painful and will enable you to squeeze out of a hold or grab and strike with a more deadly technique.

70

71

72

Front Knee

73. A knee to the groin is very effective. Use your hips to add thrust to the blow.

Round Knee

74. This works in the same way as the roundhouse kick. Come around using your body momentum to generate maximum power.

73   **74**

HEAD

Front

75. When someone grabs you, pinning your arms to the side...

76. ...use the top of your head (right at the hairline) to smash your attacker's face.

75   **76**

Back

77. When grabbed from the rear. . .

78. . . .jerk the back of your head into his face.

77   **78**

Other Weapons

In Japanese, the word "karate" means "empty hand." There will seldom be a time, however, when you will be completely empty handed. You probably have weapons of all kinds on your person in addition.

Men usually carry pens, pencils, and change in their pockets. Women will have combs, brushes, car keys, and the like in their purses.

In this chapter we will cover eight other weapons you probably have at your disposal whenever you go out of the house.

One word of caution. In these examples, a lot depends on your ability to follow up with an effective technique. If you don't have the skills to do that quickly and powerfully, you should probably let the assailant have your wallet without a fight. It's not worth your life.

On the other hand, if you feel sure he is going to try to physically harm you, go ahead and defend yourself to the best of your ability.

KEYS

79. Do not hold keys between the fingers as shown here. They can easily slip to one side or the other.

80. Place a key between your thumb and first finger and grip it tightly. Use the key you will need next, such as the one that unlocks your car door when you are in the parking lot or the one that unlocks your house when you are walking from your garage.

81. Use the key to thrust into an attacker's eye. . .

82. . . .or use it in a slashing motion.

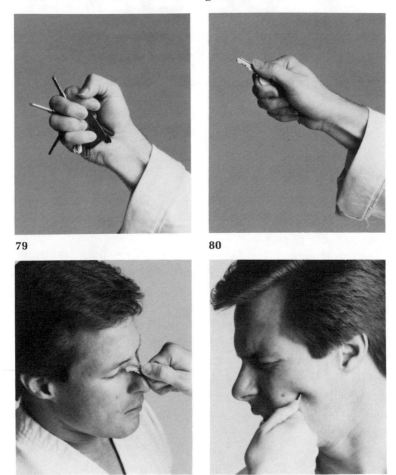

79

80

81   82

PEN

83. Hold the pen or pencil in your hand with the index finger pointing down the length of the pen or pencil. Now all you have to do is point your finger to the target.

84. A pen can be deadly if used to the right target area. Striking the eyes or throat will cause immediate pain and injury.

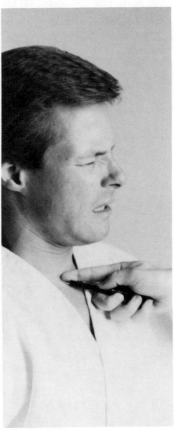

83   **84**

COMB

85. Hold the comb across the palm with the end supported by the thumb. You can use it in a slashing motion to an attacker's face or hand.

UMBRELLA

86. An umbrella or cane can easily be carried on the street and can be used to strike many vulnerable parts of an attacker's body. The face, throat, solar plexus, and groin are all targets.

85   **86**

PURSE

87. Oftentimes the very thing an assailant is after, a woman's purse, can be used as a weapon against him. A purse can be used as a distraction (that is to say, it can be put right into his face).

88. Follow up with a knee to the groin.

87   88

PACKAGES

89. You might not want to throw the new shoes you just bought at an attacker, but it is infinitely better than getting beaten or killed. Toss the package(s) right at his face.

90. Follow up with a kick to the knees or groin.

89   **90**

COINS

91. By reaching into your pockets, you are telling your opponent that you will give him some money. Throw the coins right at his eyes.

92. Follow up with a leg technique.

91   92

SPIT

93. Just the sound of it makes you curl up your nose, doesn't it? The natural reaction is to try to wipe it off immediately.

94. Now is the time for your follow-up.

93   **94**

Combination Techniques

Now let's look at some actual situations and defensive techniques. Look over the following photos, and practice the techniques shown with a partner if possible.

Remember, however, that no two situations will be exactly the same. In one instance, you might be able to use the combinations precisely as shown here and they will work wonderfully, but in another situation, your assailant might be slightly out of position and you will have to execute a different move. Use these examples more as principles of self-defense rather than as exact prescriptions of what to do in every situation.

There are obviously many more than twenty ways of grabbing someone. Remember, however, that the techniques shown here are basic principles of defense. A kick to the knee or jabbing fingers into the eyes will work in a number of instances. Practice these techniques enough and you will know what to do in almost any situation.

FRONT ATTACKS

One-Hand Grab

95. Grab.

96. Twist to the thumb side of the opponent's hand to release the hold. Use the strength of your entire arm against his thumb.

95   **96**

Two-Hand Grab

97. Grab.

98. Reach over the top with your opposite hand and clasp your hands together.

97   98

99. Pull straight up against the thumb of your attacker.
100. If he is stronger than you are, step back for more power and momentum.

99   **100**

One-Hand Grab (Lock)

101. An attacker grabs your right wrist with his right hand.

102. Use your left hand to firmly lock his hand onto your wrist.

101   102

103. Reach up and over in a clockwise direction with your right hand.

104. Grasp his wrist while still locking his hand.

105. Pushing down with your right hand will cause pain to shoot up his arm and he will drop to his knees. Note: Be sure to keep the wrist bone of his grabbing hand vertical for the best effect.

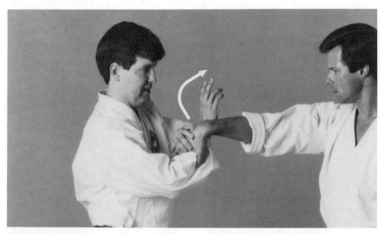

103

104

105

One-Hand Grab (Lock), Other Side

106. An attacker grabs your right wrist with his left hand.
107. Lock his hand to your wrist with your left.

106   **107**

108. Reach up and over in a counterclockwise motion with your right hand.

109. Bring your fingers over his wrist.

110. Pushing down with your right hand will cause him pain. Again, keep his wrist vertical.

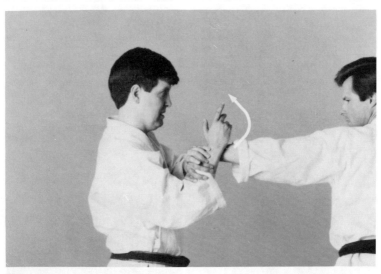

108

109

110

Choke Hold

111. Grab.

112. Reach over the top with one hand and grab your other hand coming in from the bottom.

111   **112**

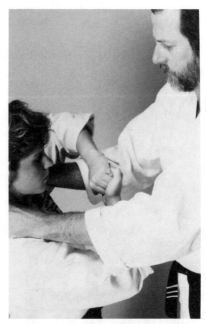

113. Close-up view.

114. Twist down on the side where your hand is on top. Use your arm underneath to push the opponent's arm up and off.

115. Keep twisting until his arm is completely off you.

113

114

115

116

Two-Hand Lapel Grab

116. Grab.

117. Cup your hands, and slap your opponent's ears. This creates a suction effect and can temporarily deafen him.

118. As a follow-up, you can use your thumbs to penetrate his eyes.

117

118

119

One-Hand Lapel Grab
119. Grab.

120. Grab his attacking hand with your right.

121. Twist your shoulders effectively, bringing him into your rising palm strike as you step out.

120

121

122

Bear Hug

122. Grab.

123. Push his hips back as you step backward.

124. Bring the knee directly into his groin.

123

124

Floor Pin

125. Hold.

126. Pull your feet up as close as possible.

127. Pull your hands out as you buck upward with your hips. This makes him release your hands to protect his face from hitting the floor.

125

126

127

128

128. As he releases your hands, roll to the side and push him off.

129. Keep rolling and pushing so he does not fall on top of you.

130. Follow up with a hammer fist to the groin.

129

130

Left Outside Block and Counter

131. The attacker is ready to grab or punch.
132. As he steps in, execute a left outside block.

131   132

133. Strike to the eyes with a spear hand.
134. Finish with a right front kick.

133   **134**

Right Outside Block and Counter

135. The attacker prepares to grab you.
136. Step to the outside and execute an outside block.

135   **136**

137. Pick the knee up high for a round kick.
138. Strike to his solar plexus or groin area.

137   **138**

REAR ATTACKS

One-Hand Grab

139. Grab.

140. Turn and block the hand off your shoulder.

141. Reverse punch to his ribs or kidneys.

139

140   **141**

Side-Hand Grab

142. Grab.
143. Grasp his sleeve for balance.

142   **143**

144

144. Turn your hips for maximum drive in the kick.

145. Side-kick to his knee joint.

146. If you are limber enough, you could follow with a higher side kick to break his ribs.

145

146

147

Two-Hand Choke
147. Grab.

148. Pick your leg up for power.

149. Drive your foot straight back into his knee.

148

149

150

Bear Hug

150. Grab.

151. Step to the right with your right foot and shift your hips to the right. This creates an open space in front of the attacker's groin.

152. Hammer-fist back into his groin.

151

152

Bear Hug (Option Two)

153. Grab.
154. Pick up your foot.

153   **154**

155. Drive a kick straight back into his knee.
156. Drop the heel hard down onto his instep.

155   **156**

157

157. Step to the side and bring your arms straight out to the front.

158. Whip a rear elbow strike into his solar plexus.

159. Finish him with a palm strike to the groin.

158

159

Arm Lock

160. Hold.

161. Turn in the opposite direction of the hold and elbow.

162. If he moves his head away or if he just falls backward, finish with a chop.

160

161

162

Head Lock

163. Hold.
164. Reach up with your right hand.

163   **164**

165

165. Grab a handful of hair. (If your attacker is bald, put your fingers into his eyes and pull back.)

166. Straighten him up to prepare for the strike.

167. Hammer-fist to the groin.

166

167

168

Head Lock with a Punch

168. If the attacker is going to punch your face, be sure to grab his punching hand from around his back.

169. Obviously, you cannot hold him for long in this position...

170. ...so you must strike quickly to the groin with a hammer fist or chop.

169

170

Full Nelson

171. Grab.

172. Position your hands in front of your forehead to counter his pressure on your neck.

171

172

173

173. Bring your heel up to his groin.

174. Reach up and peel back one or two fingers of his top hand.

175. Elbow into his face.

174

175

Defense Against Weapons

No karate instructor I know says you should try to fight someone who has a weapon. Give him your money, beg him not to hurt you, turn tail and run, do anything you have to before resorting to fighting. If he has a knife or gun, you have to assume he is an expert with that weapon and that he will use it on you.

Only if you have given him all your money and he is still threatening you should you try to disarm him. You should feel certain he is going to injure you (or worse) before you attempt to fight an armed opponent.

I have only shown you three simple knife defenses (which could easily be applied to a stick or club) because I do not want to be responsible for leading you to believe you can defend yourself against a gun just by looking at a few photographs in a book.

Downward Knife Attack

176. The opponent comes down with knife.
177. Execute a rising X-block.

176   **177**

178

178. Close-up.

179. Grab the wrist with your top hand.

180. Move to the side and use the attacker's downward momentum to guide the knife back into his body.

179   **180**

Straight-In Knife Attack

181. Do an X-block as he stabs.
182. Close-up.

181   **182**

183. Push his hand to the right as you scoop under with your right hand. Note how the thumb has captured the wrist.

184. Slipping your hands around his, step out to the left to execute a wrist lock/throw.

183   184

Back and Forth Slash

185. The attacker prepares to slash at you.
186. Wait until he has gone past you.

185   **186**

187. On his way back (on the weak swing to his rear), block with both arms.

188. Keep hold of the arm with the knife and elbow to the face.

187   **188**

Precautions

Perhaps the best self-defense weapon you have is your self-confidence. The way you walk, stand, and move can radiate calm and confidence. People who seem unaware of their surroundings and amble along daydreaming are perceived as prime targets by muggers. Police studies confirm that body movement can constitute an "assault potential" that criminals can read as a sign to move in.

Martial artists, as a rule, move in a strong but relaxed manner. They walk in a positive way as if they had a destination in mind. The mugger won't necessarily suspect they know karate, but he will probably think twice before attacking and pick an easier target.

Many people, however, have a difficult time exuding that kind of self-confidence because they feel that they couldn't seriously defend themselves. They walk the streets in paranoia. Now a little paranoia is good because it keeps you on your toes, but gaining more confidence in your abilities is the question we want to address here.

The only reason someone will attack you is because he thinks he is going to win. He doesn't expect you to be able to defend yourself. You have the element of surprise on your side, and he is vulnerable because of his overconfidence.

Remember that your face, especially your eyes, mirrors your emotions. When you are nervous or frightened, such emotions are reflected in the way you look at someone. When confronted by potential violence, try to keep your face expressionless and your eyes watchful. (It's impossible to appear confident if your eyes show fear and your facial muscles are twitching.)

Although fear can often paralyze us, it can have positive benefits as well. It can get us ready psychologically for quick action, whether it is an attack or a hasty retreat. Again, let me emphasize that running or talking your way out of a fight is not a coward's way out. Instead, it can be a sign of maturity and wisdom.

The best way to control your fear before you have to act is to try to control your breathing. Breathe calmly and deeply. Try not to hyperventilate.

If you decide you will have to fight instead of run away, do so with a loud shout or yell. Martial artists call their yell a "kiai" and bring up breath from the diaphragm to make an explosive and arresting shout. Besides unnerving your opponent, a yell tends to focus your energy and tighten your entire body so you are less likely to be hurt if hit.

As you practice the techniques in this book, imagine yourself in various real-life situations. The more mentally prepared you can be, the better. As you go about your daily activities, think defensively. Be aware of yourself and your surroundings.

When walking, stay away from parked cars, doorways, hedges, and other places an assailant might hide. Walk facing oncoming traffic to lesson the chance of a car pulling up behind you unnoticed. *Don't* jog with a set of headphones on since you'll never hear that mugger (or German shepherd) coming up on you.

Stay alert—even in your own neighborhood. A third of street muggings occur within four blocks of one's home.

Traveling with companions cuts your risk of attack by at least 80 percent. Muggers prefer a lone target. Coordinate schedules with a friend for shopping trips or recreation whenever possible.

Avoid stairwells and public rest rooms when you can. Be cautious about entering an elevator with a lone stranger. If you are frightened or threatened, push the alarm button and as many floors as possible. The alarm may frighten him and you will have a chance to get off at the next floor.

Lock yourself inside your car when driving. Be overly cautious and park your car under a light even if it is day and you may not return until after dark. Always look into your car and behind the front seat before entering. Lock your valuables in the trunk and out of sight. Leave only your car ignition key with the parking lot attendant.

Have your keys ready before you get to your car or front door and carry them as I have already shown you. Never hitchhike or accept a ride from a stranger.

Pickpockets abound at sporting events, theaters, and supermarkets—anywhere crowds gather. The safest place for a man's wallet is in his front pants pocket. If it won't fit there, carry it sideways in your rear pocket so it is harder to slip out. Women should never leave their purse unattended in a shopping cart or on a store counter. It only takes a second for someone to grab it.

If you should lose your keys, have your locks changed immediately. Many people keep their doors locked (a double-cylinder deadbolt is best) but forget to lock their windows. Lock your garage as securely as your house or a burglar may use your own tools to gain entry into your home.

Despite the fact that most people know not to allow a stranger into their home to make a phone call, the police are constantly filing robbery or rape reports on people who forget that simple rule. Always request a salesman or repairman to show identification; if you didn't request his services, call his company to verify his identity before admitting him.

Make your house look occupied when you are not at home. Have a neighbor collect mail and newspapers. Put your lights on a timer. Etch identification on nondetachable parts of your TVs, cameras, guns, and appliances.

IF CONFRONTED

Let's say you pull up to the drugstore, stop in the handicapped parking spot (I know you'd never do that, but this is an example), leave your motor running and dash into the store for a tube of toothpaste. When you return and drive off, you discover that someone has entered your car and is hidden behind your seat.

You have been taken hostage in your own car. Usually you can't tell if the intruder really intends to use a weapon on you. It is likely that he is only using it to intimidate you into giving him what he wants. He is probably as frightened as you are; by provoking him, you may cause him to react by harming you even though that was not his original intention.

That same principle applies if you confront a burglar in your home. He is excited and possibly on drugs. Assure him you will cooperate fully. You want to keep him calm to prevent violence.